March of America Facsimile Series

Number 46

Journal of
Captain Thomas Morris

Thomas Morris

Journal of
Captain Thomas Morris
from Miscellanies in Prose and Verse
by Thomas Morris

ANN ARBOR

UNIVERSITY MICROFILMS, INC.

A Subsidiary of Xerox Corporation

Foreword

"The Journal of Captain Thomas Morris," although written in 1764, was not printed until Morris collected several of his writings and published them as *Miscellanies in Prose and Verse* in London in 1791. Morris came to America in 1758 as a lieutenant in His Majesty's Seventeenth Regiment of Infantry and served at Louisbourg with Lord Jeffrey Amherst. At the time of the mission described in his "Journal" he was under the command of Lieutenant Colonel John Bradstreet, whose assignment it was to crush the resistance of the Indians of the Great Lakes area after Pontiac's uprising in 1763.

Unfortunately, Bradstreet had a vainglorious ambition to subdue the Indians singlehandedly without firing a shot and attempted to make treaties for which he had no authorization. The assignment he gave Morris to receive the submission of the Indians of the Illinois country was utterly unrealistic, since he failed to appreciate that the wilderness through which Morris had to travel with only a small company of Indians and white men was occupied by hostile Indians under Pontiac's domination.

Morris was saved from death on several occasions by the intervention of French-Canadian interpreters and once by Pontiac himself, who ruled that the life of an ambassador was sacred. Pontiac's followers, however, made repeated efforts to kill Morris. On his arrival at the Miami village, he was preserved by the happy accident that he stayed in the canoe, reading *Antony and Cleopatra* from a copy of Shakespeare's plays given him by an Indian chief, while the rest of his party were greeted by most of the village, brandishing tomahawks and other weapons. This show of hostility resulted from the arrival of members of the Shawnee and Delaware tribes with war belts. Almost simultaneously Bradstreet was making an invalid treaty with a deputation from these same tribes.

The implacable hostility of the Indians he encountered forced upon Morris the realization that he could not fulfill his orders to deliver Bradstreet's letter to the French commandant at Fort Chartres, and he reluctantly returned to Detroit, from which he sent his diary on to Bradstreet. Morris' mission was a failure, but his firsthand experience of the treachery of the Shawnee and Delaware tribes confirmed reports that Bradstreet received of raids on the frontier and, more important, it made clear to General Gage, to whom Bradstreet forwarded the diary, that Pontiac retained powerful influence among the Great Lakes tribes. The brilliant military campaign of Colonel Henry Bouquet was the effective means of subduing the Delawares and their allies, but Pontiac himself was a threat to peace for some time to come.

Morris' "Journal" has been reprinted with a brief introduction by Reuben G. Thwaites in *Early Western Travels*, I (Cleveland, 1904). His mission and its part in Pontiac's war is discussed in Francis Parkman, *The Conspiracy of Pontiac* (Boston, 1851) and Howard H. Peckham, *Pontiac and the Indian Uprising* (Princeton, 1947). Mr. Peckham has reprinted the diary upon which Morris based his "Journal" in *Old Fort News*, VI (1941), published by the Allen County-Fort Wayne Historical Society.

MISCELLANIES

IN

PROSE AND *VERSE.*

Capt.ⁿ Thoˢ Morris.

MISCELLANIES

IN

PROSE AND VERSE.

BY

CAPTAIN THOMAS MORRIS.

LONDON:

PRINTED FOR JAMES RIDGWAY, NO. 1, YORK-STREET,
ST. JAMES'S-SQUARE.

1791.

PREAMBLE.

SOME reafon perhaps ought to be affigned for my troubling the public with the following narrative. I fhall fatisfy thofe who may be of that opinion both with refpect to it and the other writings contained in this volume. The truth is this : the Journal had lain for many years in a cheft among other papers, unfeen either by myfelf or my friends. But on a late unfuccefsful event, I thought that, for the benefit of my children, I ought to attempt to repair the injury I had done them by my fpeculations, and as every one who knew the

ftory

ftory of my adventures in America, allowed
that I had a claim on government, I determined to make it.   I therefore drew up a memorial to his Majefty, fetting forth, that my
grandfather, my father, and myfelf had all
been captains in the 17th regiment of foot,
and my uncle Lieutenant Colonel to that regiment, &c.   To this I annexed the following Journal.   But having in vain fought a
mediator between Majefty and me, I dropt all
thoughts of the memorial.   It happened foon
after that I entreated a refpectable gentleman
of my acquaintance, a man of letters in whofe
judgment I place implicit faith, to criticife
my tranflation of Racine's Phædra.   This he
very kindly undertook, and even fpoke to
Mr. Harris concerning it, who, with great
politenefs, offered me his theatre, if a princi-
pal performer, whom he named, would un-
dertake the chief character.   I read the play
to that performer; but the length of fome of
the fpeeches, though fhortened as far as my

own

own judgment would permit, its being a tranflation, though of the fineft tragedy the French can boaft; the extravagant encomiums which I lavifhed on Mademoifelle Dumènil, whofe manner of acting I wifhed her to imitate, &c. &c. &c. made her lukewarm, when I wanted her to be an enthufiaft: fo that defign was dropped. One day, however, previous to this, when the gentleman, whom I have mentioned, had been employed in examining the original, while I read the tranflation; at the conclufion of the bufinefs, I faid: "I have here an attempt at an ode; " 'tis a new fancy of mine: 'tis in honour of " the national affembly of France." He read it, and defired that it might be publifhed in a newfpaper: and he afterwards encouraged me to publifh three more, which, together with the firft, are in this volume, and alfo another, not publifhed before. I then read to him fome remarks on the poetical elocution of the theatre, and on the manner of acting tragedy;

gedy: thefe he likewife advifed me to publifh in a volume, together with the odes
and other pieces of poetry. Some time after
I fpoke by accident of my memorial and
journal. He was furprifed at my account of
an adventure which, in the courfe of fifteen
years acquaintance, he had never heard me
mention. After taking it home and reading
it, he advifed me to print the Journal with
my odes, &c. to complete the volume; for
though neither the volume nor the Journal, as
he faid, might be of ufe to me, they might,
poffibly, fome time or other, procure a friend
or protector to one of my children. I have
followed his advice. This is a plain and fimple tale, accounting for my prefumption in
offering to the public an old ftory relating to
one whofe wifh ufed to be, to lie concealed
in domeftic life; a wifh, in which he has been
amply gratified by the very obliging filence
of fome of his neareft connexions.

JOURNAL

JOURNAL

OF

CAPTAIN THOMAS MORRIS,

OF

His Majesty's XVII Regiment of Infantry.

GENERAL Bradftreet, who commanded an
army fent againft thofe Indian nations who
had cut off feveral Englifh garrifons, of which we
had taken poffeffion after the furrender of Canada,
having too haftily determined to fend an officer to
take poffeffion alfo of the Ilinois country in his
Britannic Majefty's name, fent his Aid de Camp to
found me on the occafion. His Aid de Camp de-
ʳed me to recommend fome officer with qualities he
ᵈᵉ.cribed. I named every one that I could recol-

lect;

lect; but he always anfwered me fhortly: " No,
" no; he won't do." I then began to fufpect that
he might have a defign on myfelf. Accordingly I
faid: " If I thought my fervices would be accept-
" able"——He interrupted me: " That is what is
" wanted." I replied: " Why did you not fay fo
" at firft?" He faid, with an oath: " It is not a
" thing to be afked of any man." I anfwered: " If
" the General thinks me the propereft perfon, I am
" ready." I was immediately conducted to the
General; and while I was at dinner with him, he
faid, in his frank manner: " Morris, I have a
" French fellow here, my prifoner, who expects to
" be hanged for treafon; he fpeaks all the Indian
" languages, and if you think he can be of ufe to
" you, I'll fend for him, pardon him, and fend him
" with you." I anfwered: " I am glad you have
" thought of it, Sir; I wifh you would." The
prifoner, whofe name was Godefroi, was accordingly fent for; and, as foon as he entered the tent, he
turned pale, and fell on his knees, begging for mercy.
The General telling him that it was in his power to
hang him, concluded with faying: " I give thee thy
" life; take care of this gentleman." The man
expreffed

expreſſed a grateful ſenſe of the mercy ſhewn him, and proteſted that he would be faithful : and indeed his behaviour afterwards proved that he was ſincere in his promiſe.   As General Bradſtreet had pardoned him on my account, he conſidered me as his diliverer.   Little minds hate obligations ; and thence the tranſition is eaſy to the hatred of their benefactor : this man's ſoul was of another make, and, though in a low ſtation, a noble pride urged him to throw a heavier weight of obligation on him to whom he thought he was indebted for his liberty, if not his life ; and I had the ſingular ſatisfaction of owing thoſe bleſſings to one who fancied he owed the ſame to me.

While I was preparing to ſet out, the boats being almoſt loaden with our proviſions and neceſſaries, the Aid de Camp told me, that if the Indian deputies, who were expected to arrive at the camp that evening, did not come, the Uttawaw village, where I was to lie that night, would be attacked at three o'clock in the morning ; " but that," added he, " will make no difference in your affairs."   I was aſtoniſhed that the General could think ſo : but I made no reply to him, and we talked of other mat-

ters.

ters. However, as I was ſtepping into my boat, ſome canoes appeared, and I came on ſhore again, and found they were the Indian deputies who were expected. This I thought a very happy incident for me ; and having received proper powers and inſtructions I ſet out in good ſpirits from Cedar Point, in Lake Erie, on the 26th of Auguſt, 1764, about four o'clock in the afternoon, at the ſame time that the army proceeded for Detroit. My eſcort conſiſted of Godefroi, and another Canadian, two ſervants, twelve Indians, our allies, and five Mohawks, with a boat in which were our proviſions, who were to attend us to the ſwifts of the Miamis river, about ten leagues diſtant, and then return to the army. I had with me likewiſe Warſong, the great Chippawaw chief, and Attawang, an Uttawaw chief, with ſome other Indians of their nations, who had come the ſame day to our camp with propoſals of peace. We lay that night at the mouth of the Miamis river.

I was greatly delighted on obſerving the difference of temper betwixt theſe Indian ſtrangers and thoſe of my old acquaintance of the five nations. Godefroi was employed in interpreting to me all their

pleaſantries ;

pleafantries; and I thought them the moft agreeable
ralliers I had ever met with. As all men love thofe
who refemble themfelves, the fprightly manners of
the French cannot fail to recommend them to thefe
favages, as our grave deportment is an advantage to
us among our Indian neighbours; for it is certain
that a referved Englifhmen differs not more from a
lively Frenchman than does a ftern Mohawk from a
laughing Chippawaw. The next day (27th) we
arrived at the Swifts, fix leagues from the mouth of
the river, and the Uttawaw chief fent to his village
for horfes. Soon after a party of young Indians
came to us on horfeback, and the two Canadians and
myfelf having mounted, we proceeded, together with
the twelve Indians my efcort, who were on foot,
and marched in the front, the chief carrying Englifh
colours, towards the village, which was two leagues
and a half diftant. On our approaching it, I was
aftonifhed to fee a great number of white flags
flying; and, paffing by the encampment of the
Miamis, while I was admiring the regularity and
contrivance of it, I heard a yell, and found myfelf
furrounded by Pondiac's army, confifting of fix
hundred favages, with tommahawks in their hands,

who

who beat my horfe, and endeavoured to feparate me
from my Indians, at the head of whom I had placed
myfelf on our difcovering the village. By their
malicious fmiles, it was eafy for me to guefs their
intention of putting me to death. They led me up
to a perfon, who ftood advanced before two flaves
(prifoners of the Panis nation, taken in war and
kept in flavery) who had arms, himfelf holding a fu-
fee with the butt on the ground. By his drefs, and
the air he affumed, he appeared to be a French officer : I afterwards found that he was a native of old
France, had been long in the regular troops as a
drummer, and that his war-name was St. Vincent.
This fine dreffed half French, half Indian figure
defired me to difmount; a bear-fkin was fpread on
the ground, and St. Vincent and I fat upon it, the
whole Indian army, circle within circle, ftanding
round us. Godefroi fat at a little diftance from us ;
and prefently came Pondiac, and fquatted himfelf,
after his fafhion, oppofite to me. This Indian has
a more extenfive power than ever was known among
that people ; for every chief ufed to command his
own tribe : but eighteen nations, by French in-
trigue, had been brought to unite, and chufe this man
                                                    for

for their commander, after the Englifh had conquer-
ed Canada ; having been taught to believe that,
aided by France, they might make a vigorous pufh
and drive us out of North America. Pondiac afked
me in his language, which Godefroi interpreted,
" whether I was come to tell lies, like the reft of
" my countrymen." He faid, " That Ononteeo
" (the French king) was not crufhed as the Englifh
" had reported, but had got upon his legs again,"
and prefented me a letter from New Orleans, direct-
ed to him, written in French, full of the moft im-
probable falfehoods, though beginning with a truth.
The writer mentioned the repulfe of the Englifh
troops in the Miffiffippi, who were going to take
poffeffion of Fort Chartres, blamed the Natchez
nation for their ill conduct in that affair, made our
lofs in that attack to be very confiderable, and concluded with affuring him, that a French army was
landed in Louifiana, and that his father (the French
king) would drive the Englifh out of the country.
I began to reafon with him ; but St. Vincent hurried me away to his cabin ; where, when he talked
to me of the French army, I afked him if he
though me fool enough to give credit to that account ;

count ; and told him that none but the fimple Indians could be fo credulous.   Attawang, the Uttawaw chief, came to feek me, and carried me to his
cabin.   The next day (28th) I went to the grand
council, and addreffed the chiefs.   When I mentioned that their father, the king of France, had ceded
thofe countries to their brother the king of England,
(for fo the two kings are called by the Indians) the
great Miamis chief ftarted up and fpoke very loud,
in his fingular language, and laughed.   Godefroi
whifpered me, that it was very lucky that he received my intelligence with contempt and not anger,
and defired me to fay no more, but fit down, and
let my chief fpeak ; accordingly I fat down, and he
produced his belts, and fpoke.   I have called the
Miamis tongue a fingular language ; becaufe its has
no affinity in its found with any other Indian language which I have heard.   It is much wondered
whence this nation came ; who differ as much from
all the other nations in their fuperftitious practices,
as in their fpeech, and manner of encamping.   As
they left the Uttawaw villages before me on their
way home, we traced their encampments, where we
faw their offerings of tobacco, made by every indi-
vidual

vidual each morning, ranged in the niceft order, on long flips of bark both on the fhore, and on rocks in the river. They carry their God in a bag, which is hung in the front of their encampment, and is vifited by none but the prieft; if any other perfon prefumes to advance between the front of the encampment and that fpirit in the bag, he is put to death: and I was told that a drunken French foldier, who had done fo, was with great difficulty faved. "When the council was over, St. Vincent changed his note, and told me that if I could enfure to him his pardon, he would go to Detroit. I anfwered him, " that it was not in my power to promife it." However, as I found that I could not well do without him, I contrived to make him my friend. Pondiac faid to my chief: " If " you have made peace with the Englifh, we have " no bufinefs to make war on them. The war-belts " came from you." He afterwards faid to Godefroi : " I will lead the nations to war no more ; " let'em be at peace, if they chufe it: but I my- " felf will never be a friend to the Englifh. I " fhall now become a wanderer in the woods; and " if they come to feek me there, while I have an ar-

C   " row

" row left, I will fhoot at them." This I imagined
he faid in defpair, and gave it as my opinion, that he
might eafily be won to our intereft; and it afterwards proved fo. He made a fpeech to the chiefs,
who wanted to put me to death, which does him
honour; and fhews that he was acquainted with the
law of nations: " We muft not," faid he, " kill
" ambaffadors: do we not fend them to the Flat-
" heads, our greateft enemies, and they to us? Yet
" thefe are always treated with hofpitality." The
following day (29th) the Mokawk, who commanded the Indians in the provifion-boat, ftole away,
without taking my letter to General Bradftreet, as
he had been ordered, having, the night before, rob-
bed us of almoft every thing, and fold my rum (two
barrels) to the Uttawaws. The greater part of the
warriors got drunk; and a young Indian drew his
knife, and made a ftroke at me; but Godefroi feized
his arm, threw him down, and took the knife from
him. He certainly faved my life, for I was fitting,
and could not have avoided the blow though I faw it
coming. I was now concealed under my matrefs, as
all the young Indians were determined to murder me;
was afterwards obliged to put on Indian fhoes and
                                                    cover

cover myself with a blanket to look like a favage, and escape by fording the river into a field of Indian corn with St. Vincent, Godefroi, and the other Canadian. Pondiac asked Godefroi, who returned to the village to fee what was going on, "what he "had done with the Englifh man." And being told, he faid, "you have done well." Attawang came to fee me, and made his two fons guard me. Two Kickapoo chiefs came to me, and spoke kindly, telling me that they had not been at war with the Englifh for feven years. Two Miamis came like-wife, and told me that I need not be afraid to go to their village. A Huron woman however abufed me becaufe the Englifh had killed her fon. Late at night I returned to Attawang's cabin, where I found my fervant concealed under a blanket, the Indians having attempted to murder him ; but they had been prevented by St. Vincent. There was an alarm in the night, a drunken Indian having been feen at the fkirt of the wood. One of the Dela-ware nation, who happened to be with Pondiac's army, paffing by the cabin where I lay, called out in broken Englifh : "D——d fon of a b——ch." All this while I faw none of my own Indians : I be-

C 2   lieve

lieve their fituation was almoft as perilous as my
own. The following day (30th) the Miamis and
Kickapoos fet out on their return home, as provifions were growing fcarce. An Indian, called the
little chief, told Godefroi that he would fend his fon
with me, and made me a prefent of a volume of
Shakefpear's plays; a fingular gift from a favage.
He however begged a little gun-powder in return, a
commodity to him much more precious than dia-
monds. The next day (31ft) I gave Attawang, who
was going to Detroit, a letter for General Bradftreet, and to one of my fervants whom I fent along
with this chief, I gave another for his Aid de Camp.
And now, having purchafed three horfes and hired
two canoes to carry our little baggage, I fet out once
more, having obtained Pondiac's confent, for the
Ilinois country, with my twelve Indians, the two
Canadians, one fervant, St. Vincent's two flaves, and
the little chief's fon and nephew. There was
fcarcely any water in the channel of the river, ow-
ing to the great drought, fo that the canoes could
hardly be dragged along empty in fome places. We
paffed by the ifland where is Pondiac's village, and
arrived at a little village confifting of only two
pretty

pretty large cabins, and three small ones, and here
we encamped : that is, we lay on the ground; and as
a diftinguifhed perfonage, I was honoured by having
a few fmall branches under me, and a fort of bafket-
work made by bending boughs with their ends fixed
in the earth, for me to thruft my head under to avoid
the mufketoes or large gnats with which that country
is infefled. The day following (Auguft 1ft) arrived
St. Vincent and Pondiac. The latter gave the former
the great belt, forty years old, on which were de-
fcribed two hundred and ten villages. St. Vincent
joined us, and we fet forward, and arrived at another
village of the Uttawaws, the laft of their villages
we had to pafs. One of the chiefs of this village
gave me his hand, and led us into the cabin for
ftrangers, where was Katapelleecy, a chief of very
great note, who gave his hand to all my fellow-
travellers, but not to me. This man was a famous
dreamer, and told St. Vincent that he had talked
with the great fpirit the preceding night ; and had he
happened to dream any thing to my difadvantage the
night I lay there, it had been over with me. The
Indian who gave me his hand, went into the upper
range of beds, and came down dreffed in a laced fcar-
                                                    let

let coat with blue cuffs, and a laced hat. I wondered more at the colour of the cloaths than at the fine-
ry; and was told that it was a prefent from the Englifh, and that this Indian had conducted Sir Willi-
am Johnfon to Detroit. The next morning (2d)
he told me the Englifh were liars; that if I fpoke
falfehoods he fhould know it, and afked why the
General defired to fee the Indians at Detroit, and if
he would cloathe them. I affured him that the
General fought their friendfhip; and gave him, at
his own requeft, a letter of recommendation to him.
We then continued our route towards the Miamis
country, putting our baggage into the canoes, but
the greater part of us went by land, as the water was
fo fhallow, that thofe who worked the canoes were
frequently obliged to wade and drag them along.
We met an Indian and his wife in a canoe returning
from hunting; and bought plenty of venifon ready
dreffed, fome turkeys, and a great deal of dried fifh
for a fmall quantity of powder and fhot. The following day (3d) we were over-taken by Pondiac's
nephew and two other young Uttawaws, who, with
the Chippawaws before-mentioned, made the party
twenty-four. We met an Indian who, as we afterwards

wards found, had been defpatched to Pondiac **with** belts from the Shawanefe and Delawares ; but **he** would not ftop to talk to us. This day I faw **made** the moft extraordinary meal to which I ever was or ever can be witnefs. Till thefe laft named Indians joined us we had killed nothing but a very **large** wild cat, called a pichou, which indeed was **very** good eating : but this day we cat two deer, fome wild turkeys, wild geefe, and wild ducks, befides **a** great quantity of Indian corn. Of the wild **ducks** and Indian corn we made broth; the Indians **made** fpoons of the bark of a tree in a few minutes, **and,** for the firft time, I eat of boiled wild duck. **When** we marched on after dinner, I could perccive **no** fragments left. What an Indian can eat is fcarcely credible to thofe who have not feen it. Indeed **the** Frenchmen, who had been ufed to favage life, **ex-** preffed their aftonifhment at the quantity which **had** been devoured. The next day (4th) we found **plen-** ty of game, having fufficient time to hunt for **it, as** the canoes were for the greateft part of the day **drag-** ged along, there not being water fufficient to **float** them. The day after (5th) we met an Indian **on a** handfome white horfe, which had been General

Braddock's,

Braddock's, and had been taken ten years before when that General was killed on his march to Fort du Quefne, afterwards called Fort Pitt, on the Ohio. The following day (6th) we arrived at a rocky fhoal, where the water was not more than two or three inches deep, and found a great number of young Indians fpearing fifh with fticks burnt at the end and fharpened; an art at which they are very dexterous; for the chief, who fteered my canoe with a fetting-pole (no oars being ufed the whole way), whenever he faw a fifh, ufed to ftrike it through with his pole, though the end had been blunted and made as flat and broad as a fhilling, pin it to the ground, then lift it out of the water, and fhake it into the boat. I never faw him mifs a fifh which he took aim at. The day after, on the feventh of September, in the morning we got into eafy water, and arrived at the meadow near the Miamis fort, pretty early in the day. We were met at the bottom of the meadow by almoft the whole village, who had brought fpears and tommahawks, in order to def- patch me; even little children had bows and arrows to fhoot at the Englifhman who was come among them; but I had the good fortune to ftay in the

canoe,

canoe, reading the tragedy of Anthony and Cleopatra, in the volume of Shakefpear which the little chief had given me, when the reft went on fhore, though perfectly ignorant of their intention, I pufhed the canoe over to the other fide of the river, where I faw a man cutting wood. I was furprifed to hear him fpeak Englifh. On queftoning him I found he was a prifoner, had been one of Lieutenant Holmes's garrifon at the Miamis Fort, which officer the Indians had murdered, a young fquaw whom he kept having enticed him out of the garrifon under a pretext of her mother's wanting to be bled. They cut off his head, brought it to the fort, and threw it into the coporal's bed, and afterwards killed all the garrifon except five or fix whom they referved as victims to be facrificed when they fhould lofe a man in their wars with the Englifh. They had all been killed except this one man whom an old fquaw had adopted as her fon. Some years afterwards, when I lay on board a tranfport in the harbour of New York, in order to return to Europe, Sir Henry Moore, then governor of that province, came to bid me adieu, and was rowed on board by this very man among others. The man immediately recollected

D   me;

me ; and we felt, on feeing each other, what thofe only can feel who have been in the like fituations. On our arrival at the fort, the chiefs affembled, and paffed me by, when they prefented the pipe of friend-fhip ; on which I looked at Godefroi, and faid : " Mauvais augure pour moi." A bad omen for me. Nor was I miftaken ; for they led my Indians to the village, on the other fide of the water, and told me to ftay in the fort with the French inhabitants ; though care had been taken to forbid them to receive me into their houfes, and fome ftrings of wampum, on which the French had fpoken to fpare my life, had been refufed.   We wondered at this treatment, as we expected that I fhould be civilly received ; but foon learned that this change of temper was ow-ing to the Shawanefe and Delawares, a deputation of fifteen of them having come there with fourteen belts and fix ftrings of wampum ; who, in the name of their nations, and of the Senecas, declared they would perifh to a man before they would make peace with the Englifh : feven of them had returned to their villages ; five were gone to Wyaut; and three had fet out the morning I had arrived for St. Jofeph ; (a fortunate circumftance for me, for they

had

had determined to kill me). The Shawanefe and
Delawares begged of the Miamis either to put us
to death (the Indians and myfelf) or to tie us and
fend us prifoners to their villages, or at leaft to make
us return. They loaded the Englifh with the heavieft
reproaches; and added, that while the fun fhone they
would be at enmity with us. The Kiccapoos, Maf-
coutins, and Wiatanons, who happened to be at the
Miamis village declared, that they would difpatch
me at their villages, if the Miamis fhould let me
pafs. The Shawanefe and Delawares concluded their
fpeeches with faying : " This is the laft belt we fhall
" fend you, till we fend the hatchet ; which will be
" about the end of next month (October)." Doubt-
lefs their defign was to amufe General Bradftreet
with fair language, to cut off his army at Sandufky,
when leaft expected, and then to fend the hatchet to
the nations : a plan well laid ; but of which it was
my good fortune to prevent them from attempting
the execution. To return to myfelf : I remained in
the fort, and two Indian warriors (one of whom was
called Vifenlair) with tommahawks in their hands,
fiezed me, one by each arm ; on which I turned to
Godefroi, the only perfon who had not left me, and

D 2   cried

cried out to him, feeing him ftand motionlefs and pale : "Eh bien ! Vous m' abandonnez donc ?" Well then ! You give me up ? He anfwered : "Non, mon capitaine, je ne vous abandonnerai "jamais," No, my captain, I will never give you up ; and followed the Indians, who pulled me along to the water-fide, where I imagined they intended to put me into a canoe ; but they dragged me into the water. I concluded their whim was to drown me, and then fcalp me ; but I foon found my miftake, the river being fordable. They led me on till we came near their village ; and there they ftopped and ftripped me. They could not get off my fhirt, which was held by the wrift bands, after they had pulled it over my head, and in rage and defpair I tore it off myfelf. They then bound my arms with my fafh, and drove me before them to a cabin, where was a bench, on which they made me fit. The whole village was now in an uproar. Godefroi prevailed with St. Vincent, who had followed us to the water-fide, but had turned back, to come along with him ; and encouraged Pondiac's nephew and the little chief's fon to take my part. St. Vincent brought the great belt, and Pondiac's nephew fpoke. Nana-

mis,

mis, an Indian, bid Godefroi take courage, and not quit me. Godefroi told le Cygne, a Miamis chief, that his children where at Detroit ; and that, if they killed me, he could not tell what might befal them. He spoke likewise to le Cygne's son, who whispered his father, and the father came and unbound my arms, and gave me his pipe to smoke. Visenlair, upon my speaking, got up and tied me by the neck to a post. And now every one was preparing to act his part in torturing me. The usual modes of torturing prisoners are applying hot stones to the soles of the feet, running hot needles into the eyes, which latter cruelty is generally performed by the women, and shooting arrows and running and pulling them out of the sufferer in order to shoot them again and again : this is generally done by the children. The torture is often continued two or three days, if they can contrive to keep the prisoner alive -so long. These modes of torture I should not have mentioned, if the gentleman who advised me to publish my journal, had not thought it necessary. It may easily be conceived what I must have felt at the thought of such horrors which I was to endure. I recollect perfectly what my apprehensions were. I

had

had not the smallest hope of life; and I remember that I conceived myself as it were going to plunge into a gulf, vast, immeasurable; and that, in a few moments after, the thought of torture occasioned a sort of torpor and insensibility; and I looked at Godefroi, and seeing him exceedingly distressed, I said what I could to encourage him: but he desired me not to speak. I supposed that it gave offence to the savages, and therefore was silent; when Pacanne, king of the Miamis nation, and just out of his minority, having mounted a horse and crossed the river, rode up to me. When I heard him calling out to those about me, and felt his hand behind my neck, I thought he was going to strangle me out of pity: but he untied me, saying (as it was afterwards interpreted to me) I give that man his life. " If you " want meat (for they sometimes eat their prisoners) " go to Detroit, or upon the lake (meaning go face " your enemies the English) and you'll find enough. " What business have you with this man's flesh, " who is come to speak to us?" I fixed my eyes stedfastly on this young man, and endeavoured by looks to express my gratitude. An Indian then presented me his pipe; and I was dismissed by being

pushed

pufhed rudely away. I made what hafte I could to a canoe, and paffed over to the fort, having received on my way a fmart cut of a fwitch from an Indian on horfeback. Mr. Levi, a Jew trader, and fome foldiers, who were prifoners, came to fee me. Two very handfome young Indian women came likewife, feemed to compaffionate me extremely, and afked Godefroi a thoufand queftions. If I remember right, they were the young king's fifters. Happy Don Quixote, attended by princeffes ! I was never left alone, as the wretches, who ftripped and tied me, were always lurking about to find an opportunity to ftab me. I lay in the houfe of one L'Efperance, a Frenchman. The next day my Indians fpoke on their belts. The two wretches ftill fought an opportunity to kill me. The day following the Miamis returned their anfwer: " That we muft go " back ;" fhewed the belts of the Senecas, Shawanefe, and Delawares ;-gave my Indians a fmall ftring of white wampum ; and told them : " to go and in- " form their chiefs of what they had feen and heard." While the council fat I was concealed in L'Efperance's garret, as Godefroi was obliged to attend it. Being determined at all events to get into the Ilinois

country

country if poffible, St. Vincent and I agreed, that he
fhould endeavour to gain le Cygne and the young
king to attend me to Wyaut : but, in the middle of
the night, St. Vincent came and awoke me, told me
that two Frenchmen were juft arrived from St.
Jofeph, and that the Delewares, who were there,
were coming back to the Miamis village. He advifed me to fend for my chief immediately, and tell
him, for his own fafety as well as mine, to try to get
leave to go away in the morning, (for the Miamis
had appointed the next day but one for our depar-
ture). This was accordingly done, and leave obtained. I went to vifit le Cygne, who told me,
" that he would have been glad to have attended me
" to Wyaut ; but that he could not think of leading
" me to my death: for that there were fo many tomma-
" hawks lifted up there, that he fhould have trembled
" to have gone himfelf." I gave notes to Pacanne
and Pondiac's nephew, fetting forth that they had
faved my life, and entreating all Englifhmen to ufe
them kindly. (Pacanne fhewed his paper to Colonel Croghan, when he made his tour through the
Indian country, and the Colonel was pleafed to bring
him to Detroit, and, at a private meeting appointed
for

for that purpofe, fent for me, and gave me a very handfome prefent to lay at his feet). "We gave all our blankets and fhirts to thofe Indians who had done us fervice ; and hearing that the chiefs were in council, and talked of not allowing me to return with my party, but of detaining me prifóner ; and my Indians themfelves appearing uneafy, having left my money and baggage with one Capucin, a Frenchman, I hurried away about noon, vexed at heart that I had not been able to execute the orders I had received. I gave General Bradftreet's letter for Monfieur St. Ange, the French commandant at Fort Chartres, to St. Vincent, to deliver to that officer ; and figned a certificate which he was pleafed to put into my hands, fpecifying that, on many occafions, he had faved my life. Fear lent wings to my Indians this day; and we continued our march till it was quite dark, being apprehenfive of an attack. We fet out very early the next morning; and as nothing worthy of obfervation happened, my thoughts were taken up during this day's journey in admiring the fine policy of the French with refpeƈt to the Indian nations ; of which, from among a thoufand, I fhall feleƈt two remarkable inftances,

E   which

which I mention as not only worthy of imitation, but to wear out of the minds of fuch of my country-men as have good fenfe and humanity the prejudices conceived againft an innocent, much-abufed, and once happy people; who have as deep a fenfe of the juftice and benevolence of the French, as of the wrongs and haughty treatment which they have received from their prefent mafters. The firft of thefe is the encouragement given by the French court to marriages betwixt its fubjects and Indian women; by which means Lewis got admiffion into their councils, and all their defigns were known from their very birth. Add to this, that the French fo entirely won their affections by this ftep, that to this hour the favages fay, that the French and they are one people. The next inftance is, the prohibiting the fale of fpirituous liquors to Indians, under pain of not receiving abfolution : it is what the French call a *cas referve*; none but a bifhop can abfolve a perfon guilty of it. This prevented many mifchiefs too frequent among the unfortunate tribes of favages, who are fallen to our lot. From drunkennefs arife quarrels, murders, and what not? for there is nothing, however fhocking and abominable, that the

moft

innocent of that innocent people are not madly bent
on when drunk.   From impofing on the drunken
Indian in trade, abufing his drunken wife, daughter,
or other female relation, and other fuch fcandalous
practices arife ftill greater evils.   When fuch things
are done (and they are done) can we wonder that
the Indians feek revenge ?   The ill conduct of a few
diffolute pedlars has often coft the lives of thou-
fands of his Majefty's moft induftrious fubjects, who
were juft emerging from the gloom of toil and want,
to the fair profpect of eafe and contentment.   The
following day, while we were fhooting at fome turkeys, we difcovered the cabins of a hunting party on
the oppofite fide of the Miamis river ; the men were
in the woods ; but a fquaw came over to us, who
proved to be the wife of the little chief.   Godefroi
told her that I was gone to the Ilinois country
with her fon.   She informed us that the Indians
were not returned from Detroit ; and added that
there were four hundred Delawares and three hundred Shawanefe (as fhe had been told) at the Uttawaw villages, who wanted to go and fet fire to that
place.   We were fure that this piece of news about
the Shawanefe and Delawares was falfe, as the Ut-

tawaws themfelves wanted provifions : but my Indians believed it, and it ferved to bring them over at once to my way of thinking, which was, to pafs through the woods, and avoid the villages of the Uttawaws. They were all much alarmed, but in particular the Huron of Loretto. This regenerate monfter of the church, this Chriftian favage, who fpoke French fluently, had the cruelty and infolence to tell me, that as I could not march as faft as the reft, I muft take an old man and a boy (both lame) and make the beft of my way : that the chief would go with me, and he would conduct the other, who were eleven in number, and all able men. I fpoke to him with gentlenefs, and begged that he would not think of feparating from us ; on which he faid fomething, that I did not underftand, in his language which refembles that of the five nations, and of courfe was underftood by my chief, and which vexed him fo much, that he told me, " I might go " by myfelf ;" but I found means to pacify him. I now told Godefroi, who was of himfelf fo determined, that he would of courfe go with me. Upon this the Huron gave us very grofs language ; and indeed fuch ftubborn impudence I never faw. He told the

chief

chief that if he fuffered me to take my horfes with me, we fhould be difcovered, but I obtained the chief's confent to take them a little way. I then propofed going into the wood to fettle the diftribution of our provifions and ammunition; but the Huron would liften to nothing: fo leaving him and his party, confifting of ten, with my beft horfe, which he faid he would turn loofe as foon as he fhould get a little way further, I ftruck into the wood with Godefroi, the chief, the old Indian, and the Indian boy; Godefroi and myfelf on horfeback. We went North Eaft from twelve o'clock till two; from two to five we went North; and finding a pool of water, we took up our lodgings there. The next day we continued our route North, North Eaft, being as nearly as we could guefs in the courfe of the Miamis river. We endured great thirft all this day. About three o'clock we reached the fwamps, which, by the drynefs of the feafon, might have paffed for meadows, and not finding any water, about five o'clock we made a hole, two feet deep, with our hands, (for we had no kind of tool fit for that ufe) where fome tall, broad grafs grew; and getting good water, though very muddy, we made a

fire,

fire, and determined to pafs the night by the fide of
our little well. We travelled in the fwamps the following day till half an hour after one o'clock, at
which time we came to open woods, having found
water in two places on our way; but we could find
none when we wanted to repofe ourfelves at the
clofe of day. We therefore fet to work, as the day
before, and made a hole four feet deep in a place
which muft be a fwamp in the wet feafon : but it
was three hours before we got a draught of what I
might rather call watery mud than muddy water.
We were forced from want of water to ftew a tur-
key in the fat of a racoon; and I thought I had
never eaten any thing fo delicious, thought falt was
wanting : but perhaps it was hunger which made me
think fo. We heard four fhots fired very near us
juft before dark; we had a little before difcovered the
tracks of Indians, and they undoubtedly had difcovered ours, and, fuppofing us friends, fired to let
us know were they were. Thefe fhots alarmed our
chief, and he told me that I muft leave my horfes behind. I bid Godefroi drive them to fome little diftance from us, and let them go : accordingly he went
towards the place where we had left them, as if he
                                        intended

intended to do fo ; but, unknown me, to wifely defer-
red it till morning, hoping our chief would change
his mind. This night the chief, feeing me writing
by the light of the fire, grew jealous, and afked if I
was counting the trees. The next morning the
chief being a little intimidated, inftead of going Eaft
North Eaft, as agreed on the night before, in order
to draw near the Miamis river, went due North ; by
which means he led us into the moft perplexed wood
I ever faw. He had my compafs, which I afked him
for, and wanted to carry about me, as he very feldom
looked at it ; but this gave great offence, and he told
me I might go by myfelf. In fhort, he was grown
captious beyond meafure. In order to pleafe him,
we had put his pack on one of our horfes ; but we
were forced to take it off again, as a loaded horfe
could not force its way through the thick wood we
were in. I found fuch a difficulty in leading my
horfe (for it was impoffible to ride) through this
part of the foreft, that I called out to the party for
God's fake to ftop till I could fee them, or I fhould
never fee them more : at that time I could not be
more than fifteen yards behind them. They had
hurried on in purfuit of a rattle-fnake. The chief

now

now told me again, that I muſt let **my horſes go;**
but Godefroi convinced me, that I **could not reach**
Detroit without them. I therefore **reſolved, if he**
perſiſted, to quit him, to take Godefroi **with me,**
and to kill one of my horſes for a **ſupply of food,**
for we had very little ammunition **left, and no pro-**
viſions. However the chief grew good-**humoured**
by Godefroi's management; and as he **now thought**
himſelf out of danger, changed his **courſe, going**
Eaſt North Eaſt. We ſoon got into a **fine open**
wood, where there was room to drive **a coach and**
ſix. Here we halted to refreſh ourſelves **by ſmoaking**
our pipes, having nothing to eat, the **old Indian,**
who always ranged as we travelled on, having **found**
no game that morning. As I had not been **uſed to**
ſmoaking, I deſired to have ſumach leaves **only,**
without tobacco; but, after a few whiffs, **I was ſo**
giddy, that I was forced to deſiſt: probably **an emp-**
ty ſtomach was the chief cauſe of this **unpleaſant**
effect of ſmoaking. Soon after we came into **exten-**
ſive meadows; and I was aſſured that thoſe **meadows**
continue for a hundred and fifty miles, being in **the**
winter drowned lands and marſhes. By the **dryneſs**
of the ſeaſon they were now beautiful paſtures: **and**
here

here prefented itfelf one of the moft delightful pro-
fpects I ever beheld,; all the low grounds being meadow, and without wood, and all the high grounds
being covered with trees, and appearing like iflands ;
the whole fcene feemed an elyfium. Here we found
good water, and fat down by it, and made a comfort-
able meal of what the old Indian had killed, after
we left our halting-place. We afterwards continued
our route, and at five o'clock difcovering a fmall
rivulet, which gave us all, and me in particular, in-
expreffible pleafure, we made a fire by the fide of it,
and lay there all night. The day following, we
croffed the tracks of a party of men running from
the Uttawaw villages directly up into the woods,
which we imagined to be thofe of the Huron's party
who might have loft their way ; as it proved. I
laughed and joked a good deal with Godefroi on this
occafion ; for when the Huron left us, I afked in a
fneering manner, " if he had any commands, in cafe
" I fhould get before him to Detroit :" and he anfwered me in the fame tone, " if when you arrive,
" you don't find me there, you may fafely fay that I
" am gone to the devil." Soon after, to our great
joy, we fell into the path leading from the Uttawaw

F   villages

villages to Detroit, and ſtruck into a by-path to
avoid meeting Indians ; but unluckily ſtumbled on
that which led from the great path to Attawang's
village. We met three Hurons on horſeback, who
told us, that peace was concluded, that the Uttawaws
had returned the day before to their villages, and
that General Bradſtreet was to be at Cedar-Point
that night on his way to Sanduſky. One of theſe
Indians had been preſent when I was priſoner at Attawang's village ; and though I was dreſſed like a
Canadian, and ſpoke French to Godefroi to prevent
diſcovery, recollected me to be the Engliſhman he
had ſeen there. I gave him a letter from St. Vincent to Pondiac which I had promiſed to deliver.
They then took their leave of us ; and as ſoon as
they were out of ſight, we turned into the great
path, and putting our Indians on our horſes, Godefroi and I walked at a very great rate. We arrived
at the Pootiwatamy village at a quarter paſt three,
where I had the pleaſure of ſeeing Engliſh colours
flying. I wanted to avoid the village ; but the
chief, being very hungry (for we had eat nothing
that day) fell into a paſſion, and aſked what we were
afraid of. He knew he ran no riſk here. I was a
little

little vexed, and mounting my horfe bid him follow.
I went to the village, where I bought a little Indian
corn and a piece of venifon ; and then Godefroi and
I rode on till it was dark, in hopes of reaching Detroit the next day ; and finding water, made a fire
near it, and paffed the night there, having left our
fellow-travellers to fleep with the Pootiwatamies ;
who, as none of them knew me, were told by Godefroi that I was gone to the country of the Ilinoia,
and that he growing tired of the journey, and wanting to fee his children, was on his return home.
The next morning we fet out at the dawn of day ;
and, to fave ourfelves the trouble of making a raft,
took the upper road, though the journey was much
longer that way, hoping to find the river fordable,
in which we were not difappointed. We travelled
this day a great way, and our horfes were fo much
fatigued, that they were hardly able to carry us towards the clofe of the day. We found frefh horfe-
dung on the road, which Godefroi having curioufly
examined, knew that fome Indians had juft paffed
that way ; and by their tracks he was fure they were
before us. He therefore made an excufe to halt for
about an hour, endeavouring to conceal the truth

from

from me ; but I was no ſtranger to his real motive. However, about ſeven o'clock we arrived at Detroit ; whence I was fifty leagues diſtant when I left the Miamis river and ſtruck into the woods : and by the circuit I was obliged to make to avoid purſuit, I made it at leaſt fourſcore leagues, or two hundred and forty miles. The Huron and his people did not arrive till many days after, and in three different parties. They had loſt their way ; were obliged to divide themſelves into ſmall bodies in order to ſeek for game ; had ſuffered extremely by fatigue and hunger ; one having died by the way, and all the reſt being very ill when they reached Detroit. The Huron I imagined would have died. I gave him, as well as all the others, all the affiſtance in my power ; but could not help reproaching him with his barbarity to me, and reminding him, " that the " Great Spirit had protected one whom he had " abandoned, and puniſhed him who had baſely de- " ſerted his fellow-warrior." Immediately after my arrival at Detroit, I ſent an expreſs to General Brad- ſtreet, with an account of my proceedings, and to warn him of the dangerous ſituation he was in, being advanced ſome miles up the Sanduſky river, and

ſurrounded

furrounded with treacherous Indians.   The moment
he received my letter, he removed, falling down the
river, till he reached Lake Erie : by this means he
difappointed their hopes of furprifing his army.
This army however fuffered extremely afterwards,
and great numbers were loft in traverfing the defert,
many of their boats having in the night been dafhed
to pieces againft the fhore, while the foldiers were
in their tents.   The boats were unfortunately too
large to be drawn out of the water.   The centinels
gave the alarm on finding the fudden fwell of the
lake , but after infinite labour, from the lofs of
boats, a large body of men were obliged to attempt
to reach Fort Niagara by land, many of whom
perifhed.   It is worthy of remark, that, during this
violent fwell of the waters, foldiers ftood on the
fhore with lighed candles, not a breath of wind being perceived.   This phænomenon often happens.
Another curious fact refpecting the waters of thefe
lakes is, that they rife for feven years and fall for
feven years ; or in other words, there is a feven years
tide.   I have read fomewhere, that the Cafpian fea
overflows its banks once in fifteen years.   This,
however, is denied elfewhere.   But, if the former
opinion

opinion be really the case, as the American lakes and the Caspian sea are in parts of the earth almoſt oppoſite to each other, it might be worth while to enquire, whether, when they are at the loweſt in one place, they are at the higheſt in that which is oppoſite, or both riſe and fall at the ſame time?

The Natchez nation, mentioned in the letter to Pondiac, which he ſhewed me, and who were blamed by the reſt of the Indian army for having fired too ſoon on the Engliſh who were ſent to take poſſeſſion of Fort Charters by way of the Miſſiſſippi river, no doubt did it by deſign, that the troops might have an opportunity of retreating; for the French had formerly endeavoured to extirpate that nation, and had nearly ſucceeded in the undertaking, a ſmall number only having eſcaped the maſſacre. It is not probable ſuch an action could ever be forgiven; eſpecially by ſavages. This nation have a perpetual fire; and two men are appointed to watch it. It has been conjectured that their anceſtors were deſerters from the Mexicans who worſhip the ſun.

The Miamis nation, of whom I have ſpoken ſo much, and into whoſe hands I fell after leaving Pondiac's army at the Uttawaw villages, are the very

people

people who have lately defeated the Americans in three different battles; and when the laſt accounts from that country reached us, they were encamped on the banks of the Ohio, near the falls or cataracts of that river.

It may not be improper to mention, that if I could have completed the tour intended, viz. from Detroit to New Orleans, thence to New York, and thence to Detroit again, whence I ſet out, it would have been a circuit little ſhort of five thouſand miles.

DETROIT, September 25, 1764.